WORLD BOOK'S
YOUNG SCIENTIST

WORLD BOOK'S

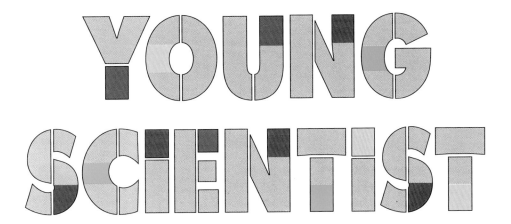

Our World in Danger

World Book, Inc.
a Scott Fetzer company
Chicago London Sydney Toronto

**Activities that have this
warning symbol require
some adult supervision!**

The quest to explore the known world and to describe its
creation and subsequent development is nearly as old as
mankind. In the Western world, the best-known creation
story comes from the book of Genesis. It tells how God
created the earth and all living things. Modern religious
thinkers interpret the Biblical story of creation in various
ways. Some believe that creation occurred exactly as
Genesis describes it. Others think that God's method of
creation is revealed through scientific investigation. *Young
Scientist* presents an exciting picture of what scientists
have learned about life and the universe.

World Book, Inc.
525 W. Monroe
Chicago, IL 60661

For information on other World Book
products, call 1-800-255-1750.

ISBN: 0-7166-6308-2
Library of Congress Catalog Card No. 95-61308

Printed in Mexico

1 2 3 4 5 6 7 8 9 10 99 98 97 96 95

Acknowledgments

The publishers of **World Book's Young Scientist** acknowledge the following photographers, publishers, agencies, and corporations for photographs used in this volume.

Cover	ZEFA Picture Library; Norman (ZEFA Picture Library)
8/9	ZEFA Picture Library; Bruce Coleman Ltd
10/11	Science Photo Library; Bruce Coleman Ltd
12/13	ZEFA Picture Library
16/17	Rod Williams (Bruce Coleman Ltd); L.C. Marigo (Bruce Coleman Ltd)
20/21	M. J. Thomas (Frank Lane Picture Agency)
22/23	L. C. Marigo (Bruce Coleman Ltd)
24/25	Loren McIntyre (Susan Griggs Agency); Elizabeth Kemf
30/31	ZEFA Picture Library
32/33	Mark Boulton (Bruce Coleman Ltd); B. Peterson (ZEFA Picture Library)
34/35	ZEFA Picture Library
36/37	Eric Crichton (Bruce Coleman Ltd)
44/45	Everts (ZEFA Picture Library)
48/49	Frank Spooner Picture Agency
50/51	ZEFA Picture Library; Greenpeace
52/53	ZEFA Picture Library
54/55	David R. Frazier

Illustrated by

Sue Barclay
Richard Berridge
John Booth
Maggie Brand
David Cook
Richard Deverell
Farley, White, and Veal
Jeremy Gower
John Lobban
Annabel Milne
Teresa O'Brien
Jeremy Pyke
Barry Rowe
Pat Tourret
Peter Visscher
Lynne Willey

Contents

8

We gather crops such as corn, wheat, and rice to feed ourselves.

We dig and drill for coal, oil, and other minerals from below the earth's surface.

Life on earth

The earth provides food and shelter for over five billion people.

There are more than five billion people living on our planet earth. The earth provides us with air to breathe, food to eat, and water to drink. It gives us the materials for homes and shelter, as well as for clothes, and it provides us with many other things that we need or enjoy. Every single one of us depends on the materials of the planet earth for life.

Every one of us needs space. We need space for a home, space in which to move around and space in which to work. We need space for farms, where we can grow food, and space for factories. We need long stretches of space to build roads and wide areas of open space for parks. People have found many ways of using the space on our planet.

We need to eat, to build homes, and to stay warm. To do these things we use the land. We farm crops and herds of animals for food. We cut down trees and other plants. We dig up coal and drill for oil. We use up the things that the earth provides. We call these things the earth's **natural resources.**

Our future

The earth is important not just to the people who are living now, whom we call the earth's **population.** When you grow up, you may have children, and your children will probably have children. They, too, will need the things the earth provides. Between the years 1990 and 2000, the population of the earth may grow by about 900 million people. By the year 2030, the population could double. Will there still be food for everyone? Will the earth be a healthy and pleasant place to live? Will there be enough clean water, and will the air be safe enough to breathe?

Many animals share the earth with us. They provide us with meat, milk, and skins.

Find out more by looking at pages **12–13**

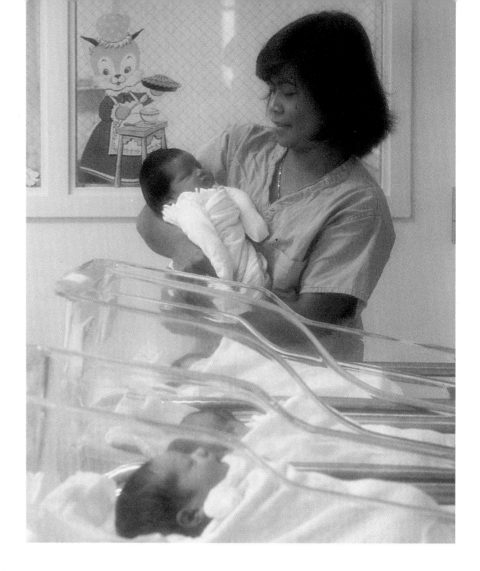

These tiny, newborn babies are kept in incubators. Inside, the babies can be given oxygen and be protected from sudden changes in temperature.

A crowded earth

For every single person alive in 1900, there are now more than three people. Today the world's population grows by nearly 90 million people every year. Why is this happening?

A longer life

The main reason for the increase is that people live longer. In the early 1900's, people who lived in North America, for example, might expect to reach their 47th birthday. Since then, **life expectancy** has increased. People eat better food. They live and work in cleaner, healthier places. And they are helped by more medicines when they become ill. Today, North Americans can look forward to their 74th birthday. Their life expectancy has increased by 27 years! Many babies who might once have died of disease as infants can now be kept alive and will grow to be healthy children.

Spreading homes

When too many people live in one place, life can become very difficult and unpleasant. In some places, there are so many people that there is not enough food or housing for everyone. Many families move to the cities, hoping to find work and homes. In time, the cities become overcrowded as more and more people arrive. More homes need to be built. Some people build their own homes using whatever materials they can find. The city spreads over more and more land. Good farming land is taken over to build houses, factories and roads. As the world's population grows, there is less and less land available for farming.

The growth of towns and cities is called urban spread. It takes up land that could be used for food crops, and also destroys the places where plants and animals live.

Spoiling the earth

For thousands of years, people hunted, fished, and farmed the land for food. They used plants to make cloth, paper, dyes, and medicines. They made tools and weapons from stone and metals. In time, they invented machines which were driven by water. Later, people learned how to power them with fuels like coal, gas, or oil. They built larger and larger cities and could reach them by road, rail, or air. They put up factories where hundreds of thousands of products could be made, like new types of clothing, furniture, and machines. And they built power stations to provide factories and homes with electricity.

Using up resources

For a long time, no one realized that all these activities were harming the earth. It was difficult to see just how quickly we were using up important natural resources like oil, coal, gas, and useful minerals. Everyone seemed to think there would always be new supplies, and few people worried about whether the resources could be saved or replaced.

Few people, too, worried about the spreading cities or about spoiling our surroundings. They did not take into account that plants and animals were disappearing as the population spread over the land. They did not realize the serious damage that they could cause the earth. They did not think about helping to save the earth and its resources, the work we now call **conservation.**

This aerial photograph of a lava quarry in Germany shows how digging for resources can destroy farmland.

Depending on each other

Do you live in the country? If so, you probably have a patch of land or a garden near your home where vegetables and other foods can be grown. But many people live in towns and cities without gardens. They depend on farmers in the countryside to grow enough food for everyone.

Protecting our crops

Farmers try to grow the best crops on their farmland. But they need to protect their crops from pests and diseases. Some farmers spray their crops with special liquids called **pesticides.** Many of these sprays are poisonous. They will kill the pests and diseases, but, unfortunately, they have other effects.

1. The mice have found a home in this field of grass, though they have to beware of owls.

2. The mice are pests because they eat the farmer's crops. The farmer has sprayed his crops with pesticide.

3. The mice eat the grain, but it does not kill them immediately.

Natural habitat

The farmer's field was a home, or **habitat,** to many living things, both plants and animals, which depend on each other in many ways. It was a place where mice, for example, found food and shelter. When the farmer plowed the land, he destroyed the wild plants that grew in the field. Animals such as the mice that fed on these plants had to go elsewhere to find food. Other animals, like owls who fed on the mice, had to move away also. What the farmer did affected not just one kind of plant or animal, but all the plants and animals living in the habitat.

Breaking the food chain

Eventually the farmer's field may once again attract mice. They will feed on grain and use the tall cereal grasses to build their nests. Then owls might return to feed on the mice. The farm cat might also eat the mice.

Plants and animals that provide food for each other are members of a food chain. If the food chain is broken, every animal in it will suffer. What do you think happens when the farmer poisons the mice?

4. A mouse that is weakened by the poison is easy prey for an owl. The owl that eats a poisoned mouse eventually dies from the poison.

5. The farmer's cat eats another poisoned mouse and dies. The farmer is pleased to be rid of the mice. But he has killed two animals which would have helped him. Owls and cats help to keep down farm pests.

Find out more by looking at
pages 12–13
         18–19

16

Some scientists are worried that the numbers of koalas may increase enormously. If this happens, the koalas' food supply, the eucalyptus tree, may run out.

Disappearing life

Can you imagine being the last person alive on the earth? You would be the last member of your animal group, or **species,** called *Homo sapiens.* Many animals and plants once found on earth are already extinct. Over time, new species developed in their place. But today, thousands of animal species and even more plants are in danger of dying out, and there is little hope that they will be replaced.

Why do animals become extinct?

The dinosaurs became extinct about 65 million years ago. There may have been a natural disaster or a change in climate that destroyed their habitat. Perhaps their food supply disappeared. Many animals face these threats today. Lion tamarins in Brazil are losing their habitat because the forest is being cut down for timber and farmland. In China, giant pandas live on a few species of bamboo. Some kinds of bamboo flower once every 100 years and then die. It may be years before the seeds grow again. Flowering occurred in the late 1970's, and hundreds of giant pandas starved. In Australia, koalas eat mainly the leaves and shoots of eucalyptus trees. If these are in short supply, the koalas starve.

Endangered plant life

Some species of plant life have become extinct because of natural causes, but the activities of human beings have endangered many more. For example, humans have cut down forests, drained wetlands, built houses, and created much pollution. As a result, some plant species have declined greatly in numbers, and others are extinct. Plants facing extinction include the black cabbage tree, the St. Helena redwood, and several California manzanitas.

In the late 1970's, large areas of bamboo in China flowered and died. Many giant pandas starved before new shoots could grow again.

The lion tamarin lives in the rain forests of eastern Brazil. It is becoming very rare, as people destroy more and more of its forest habitat.

Tropical rain forests are fast disappearing. People are cutting down the trees to make farmland and to build cities.

Animals in danger

Animal species that are in danger of dying out are called **endangered species.** People are one of the greatest threats to the survival of some animals. Many animals are endangered because of our activities. We destroy their habitats, disturb their food chains, and even hunt some of them.

Disturbing wildlife

In the past, many tigers, lions, and leopards were killed for their skins or just for sport. Many different kinds of animals are still killed by human hunters. Illegal hunters, called **poachers,** still shoot elephants and rhinoceroses for their valuable tusks and horns. Blue whales are harpooned for meat, fat or blubber, and whale-bone.

Hunting is just one way in which we disturb wildlife. Farming the land, using poisons, cutting down trees, collecting rare species—all these activities can threaten the existence of much of the world's wildlife.

Protecting wildlife habitats

Nothing can be done about the plant and animal species that are already extinct. But we can do a lot to protect those which are endangered. The governments of many countries have already passed laws against hunting endangered animals.

Project Tiger

In the early 1900's, there were many thousands of tigers in Asia. But thousands were hunted and killed. Then people cleared the forests where they lived and more died. By 1988, there were fewer than 5,000 left. There was a real danger that tigers were becoming extinct.

But the tiger story has a happy ending. A plan called Project Tiger was set up. Many countries in Asia put aside special areas of land, called "tiger reserves," where tigers could not be hunted. The remaining habitats of the tigers were protected by law. By the early 1990's, the number of tigers had increased.

tiger

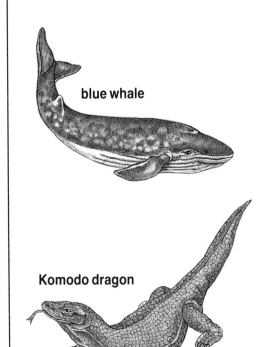

California condor

great Indian rhinoceros

blue whale

Komodo dragon

Endangered species — animals in danger

Animal	Habitat
California condor	California condors now live only in captivity.
Philippine eagle	This eagle is found in the forests of the Philippines.
Queen Alexandra's birdwing butterfly	Queen Alexandra's birdwing butterflies live in the forests of Papua New Guinea.
European lynx	This lynx was once common in Europe and northern Asia.
Mountain gorilla	Mountain gorillas inhabit the forests of east-central Africa.
Indian rhinoceros	This rhinoceros lives in reserves in northeast Nepal.
Blue whale	The oceans of the world are the home of the blue whale.
Giant panda	Giant pandas are found only in bamboo forests in the mountains of western and southwestern China.
Orangutan	The orangutan lives deep in the forests of Borneo and Sumatra.
Polar bear	Polar bears live on the cold shores of the Arctic Ocean.
Marine otter	The marine otter lives in the waters off South America.
Komodo dragon	Komodo dragons live on the islands of Indonesia.

Find out more by looking at pages **22–23**
24–25

Protecting plants

Plants are some of the living things that are most important for our survival on earth. Without plants, there would be no life on our planet. The food we eat comes from plants or from animals that eat plants. The oxygen we breathe has been formed by plants over billions of years. Even some of our building materials (such as wood) and clothing (such as cotton) come from plants.

How can we help the plant kingdom? We can stop gathering wild flowers to decorate our homes. Flowers produce the seeds which will grow into new plants, so they should be left to bloom and shed their seeds where they grow. We should try not to harm birds. They eat the fruits which contain plant seeds and scatter the seeds in their droppings. When we walk through the countryside, we should follow well-worn paths. Then we will not disturb the wildlife. We should never start fires. Fires can spread quickly, destroying everything in their path.

Wild flowers are beginning to grow on this piece of land, which had been spoiled by people. But it will be many years before the land recovers.

Protect nature

Here are six, easy-to-remember rules which will help you protect the plants and animals in the places you may visit.

Never eat wild berries, fruits, or fungi without asking an adult first. Some are poisonous!

1. Do not pick flowers.

2. Do not take birds' eggs.

3. Keep to well-worn paths.

4. Never start fires.

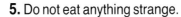

5. Do not eat anything strange.

6. Take your litter home.

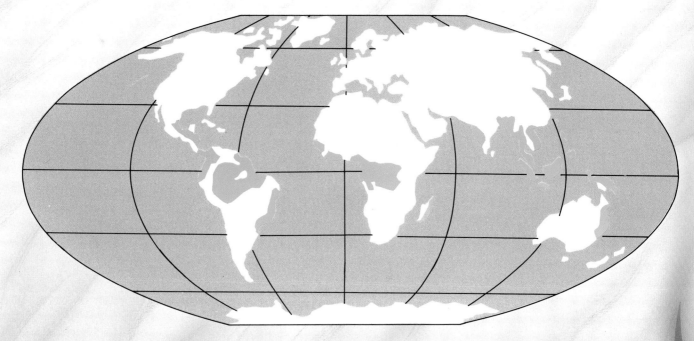

There are thick tropical rain forests near the equator in Central and South America, Africa, Asia, and on Pacific islands. About half of the world's species of plants and animals live in the tropical rain forests.

Tropical rain forests

Vast regions of the earth have plenty of sunshine and rain. This hot, wet climate makes trees and plants grow quickly, forming huge, dense forests. These are known as **tropical rain forests.** Mahogany and rosewood are kinds of trees known as hardwoods. They are some of the trees which grow well in the tropics. They provide a good habitat for animals. Many animals, such as parrots, monkeys, eagles, and bats, find food and shelter high up in the trees.

But these trees also provide us with a valuable harvest of good-quality timber. For this reason, vast stretches of forests are being cut down. Other areas are cleared to provide land for farming or for mining rich ores. More forest is cleared to make way for roads.

Meanwhile, what is happening to the plant and animal life of the forest? Many of the plants have been lost forever. Those animals which depend on the plants for food must move on to remaining parts of the forest. They will be followed by other animals in the food chain. Soon the remaining forest is crowded and unable to support all the animals that are trying to live in it.

Find out more by looking at
pages **16–17**
24–25

No protection

Much of the land that has been cleared is used for farming. But without the protection of the trees, the soil quickly dries out and breaks up in the heat and wind. After a few years, the soil is worn out, and the farmer must clear new land.

If people continue to cut down these forests as they are doing today, two-thirds of the world's tropical rain forests will have been destroyed by the year 2000. This is a serious problem because trees take in carbon dioxide, so if there are fewer trees, there will be more carbon dioxide in the air. Carbon dioxide traps heat from the sun, so the world's climate will become hotter in the future. The destruction of the rain forests is one of the world's most important conservation problems.

Machines like these claw their way through the rain forests. They are destroying about 50 million acres (20 million hectares) of rain forest each year.

Saving the forests

What can we do to help save the tropical rain forests? There are two ways to prevent them from disappearing altogether. One way is to make sure that no more trees are cut down. The other is to replant trees on forest land that has been cleared.

If we look after the forests, they can still provide us with timber. The older trees can be felled, leaving the younger trees with room to grow. This way, the forests will provide a continuous home for plant and animal life. The growing trees will use up carbon dioxide and give out oxygen. Trees can also be planted to replace those that have been cut down.

National parks

The governments of countries in South America, central Africa, and Southeast Asia have started to protect their rain forests. They have turned areas of forest into national parks, where all tree-felling and other activities that could damage the forest and its wildlife are strictly controlled.

In Brazil, people are experimenting with different types of trees to help replant the forest quickly.

Students in Vietnam are replanting an area of forest destroyed during the Vietnam War.

Putting trees back

In Vietnam, in Southeast Asia, large areas of rain forest have already been destroyed by clearance and also by war. But the Vietnamese people are beginning to replant the forests. They have planted fast-growing trees in the cleared areas. These kinds of trees are not usually found in rain forests. They do not support the same animals or plants. But as these trees grow, they provide protection for other, slower-growing plants. After many, many years, there could be new rain forests.

Putting animals back

The animal life of the rain forest is more difficult to bring back. Before they were destroyed, the forests in Vietnam provided a safe habitat for thousands of species, from tigers and elephants to tiny insects. If the replanting of the forests succeeds, it will be necessary to bring animals from other rain forests—or zoos—to restock them.

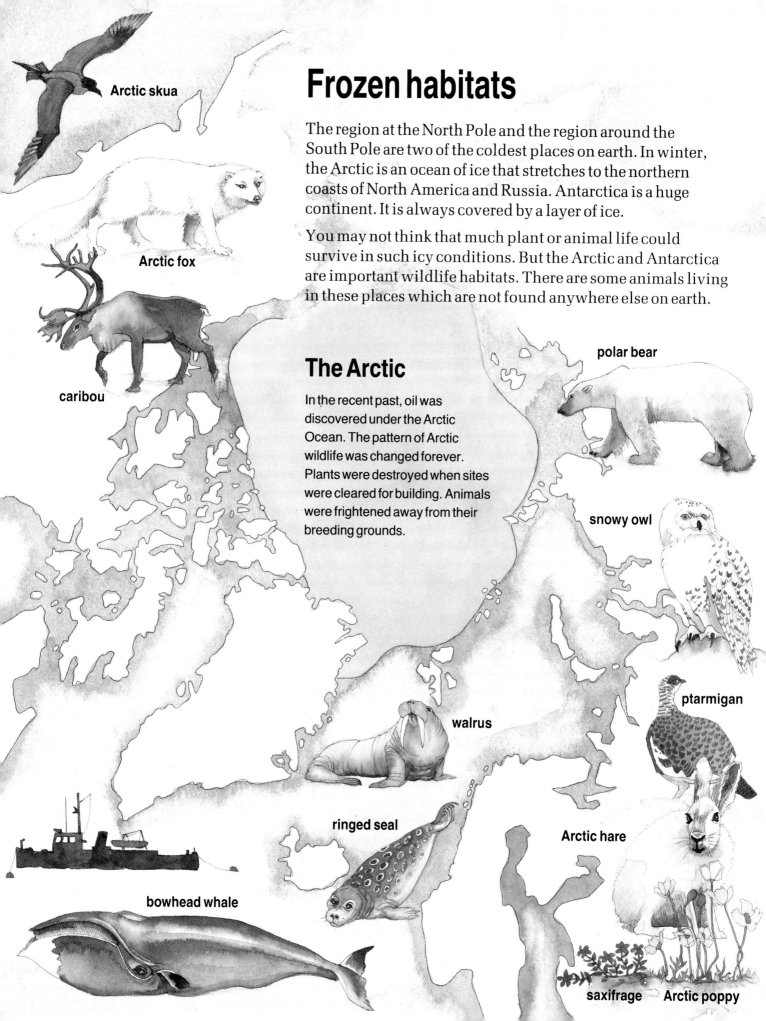

Frozen habitats

The region at the North Pole and the region around the South Pole are two of the coldest places on earth. In winter, the Arctic is an ocean of ice that stretches to the northern coasts of North America and Russia. Antarctica is a huge continent. It is always covered by a layer of ice.

You may not think that much plant or animal life could survive in such icy conditions. But the Arctic and Antarctica are important wildlife habitats. There are some animals living in these places which are not found anywhere else on earth.

The Arctic

In the recent past, oil was discovered under the Arctic Ocean. The pattern of Arctic wildlife was changed forever. Plants were destroyed when sites were cleared for building. Animals were frightened away from their breeding grounds.

Arctic skua

Arctic fox

caribou

polar bear

snowy owl

ptarmigan

walrus

ringed seal

Arctic hare

bowhead whale

saxifrage   Arctic poppy

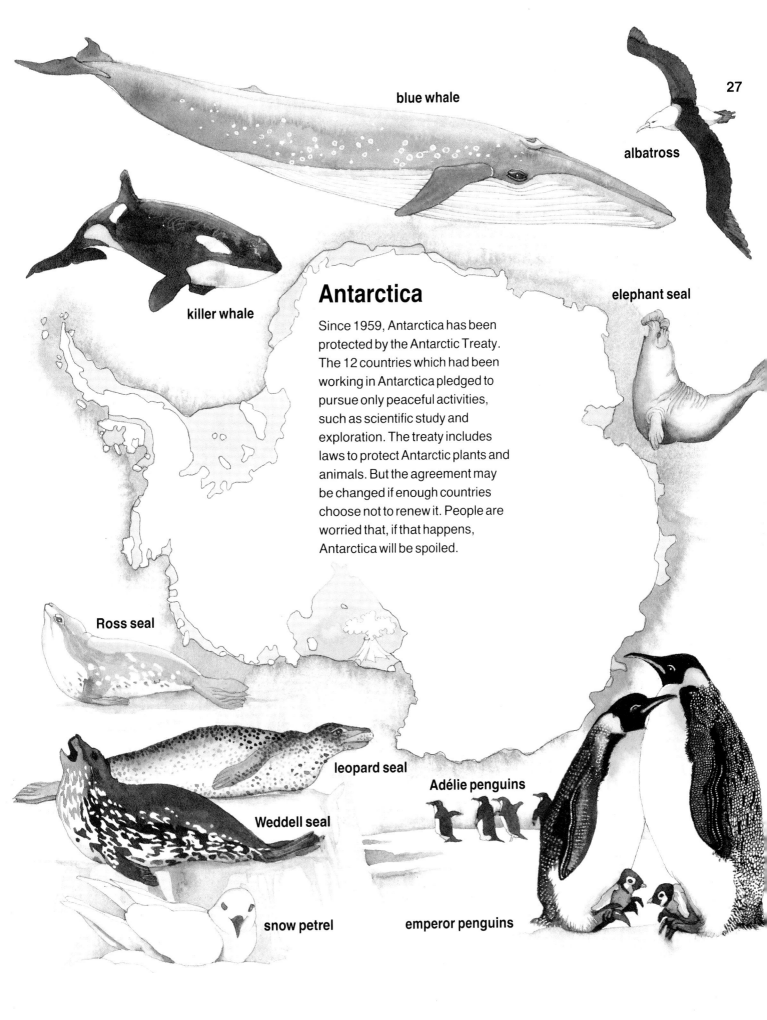

blue whale

albatross

killer whale

elephant seal

Antarctica

Since 1959, Antarctica has been
protected by the Antarctic Treaty.
The 12 countries which had been
working in Antarctica pledged to
pursue only peaceful activities,
such as scientific study and
exploration. The treaty includes
laws to protect Antarctic plants and
animals. But the agreement may
be changed if enough countries
choose not to renew it. People are
worried that, if that happens,
Antarctica will be spoiled.

Ross seal

leopard seal

Weddell seal

Adélie penguins

snow petrel

emperor penguins

Find out more by looking at pages **30–31**

The ozone layer

During the late 1970's, scientists began to notice something strange happening in the earth's atmosphere. They were surprised to see a "hole" appearing each spring in a layer of gas that surrounds the earth. This layer of gas is called the **ozone layer.**

The scientists noticed that the ozone layer appeared to be getting thinner and thinner. The problem was most serious over Antarctica. Here they found the ozone layer was thinner each spring. There are fears that the ozone layer may eventually thin out over more populated areas. Though these "holes" may be smaller than the one over Antarctica, there is enough cause for concern.

Dangerous holes

The ozone layer lies in the stratosphere, between 9 and 18 miles (15 and 30 kilometers) above the earth's surface. This layer shields us from some of the **ultraviolet rays** from the sun. These are the rays which make pale human skins become darker in sunlight. But too many ultraviolet rays can be bad for us.

During the late 1970's, scientists observed that the ozone layer over Antarctica had become thinner. Since then, it has become thinner still, allowing harmful ultraviolet rays from the sun to pass through the atmosphere.

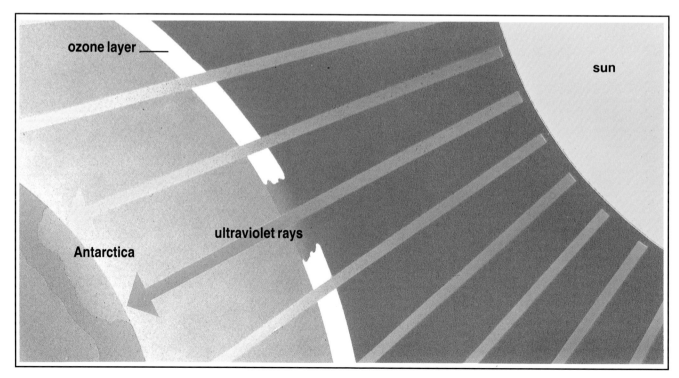

ozone layer

sun

ultraviolet rays

Antarctica

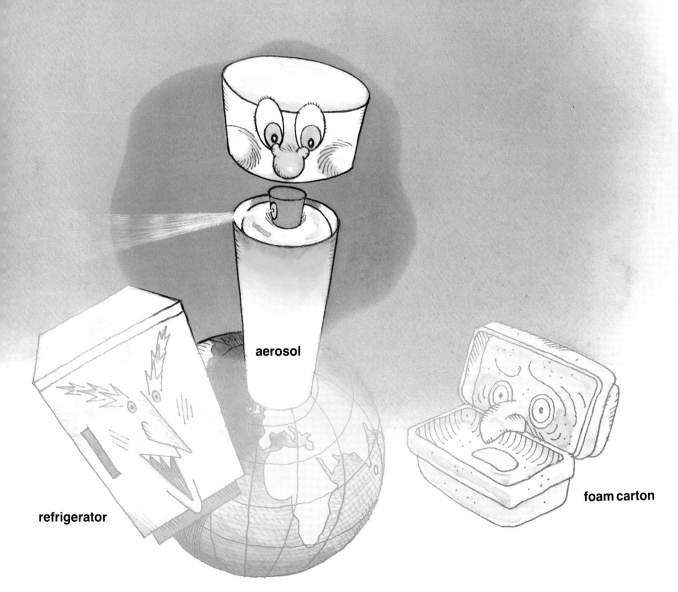

refrigerator

aerosol

foam carton

Chlorofluorocarbons (CFC's) from aerosol sprays, refrigerators, and foam cartons destroy ozone.

Harmful chemicals

No one knows for sure what is causing the ozone layer to become thinner. But we do know that certain chemicals make the ozone break down and disappear. These harmful chemicals, called **chlorofluorocarbons** (CFC's), have been used in aerosol sprays, air conditioning units and refrigerators, and to make plastic cartons and other products.

Some countries, including the United States, banned CFC sprays many years ago. Other countries have slowly followed their example. By the early 1990's, many countries agreed to end their production of CFC's. However, CFC's already in use continue to damage the ozone layer. For instance, numerous refrigerators now in use have CFC's safely contained. But when a refrigerator is thrown away or broken up, the CFC's are released into the atmosphere.

Living in a greenhouse

The world is getting warmer. If you enjoy warm weather, you may think this is good news—but it's not. Some experts say that over the last hundred years, temperatures on the earth have increased by 2.7 to 10 degrees Fahrenheit (1.5 to 5.6 degrees Celsius). The earth's atmosphere is warming up, just as if it was trapped inside a greenhouse. This warming process is often called the **greenhouse effect.**

Why is the earth warming up?

More of the sun's energy is reaching the earth's atmosphere because the ozone layer is becoming thinner. But there is another reason why the earth is warming up. When we burn fuels like coal, oil, gas, or wood, carbon dioxide is released into the atmosphere. Plants use carbon dioxide to help make their food. So tropical rain forests take in large amounts of carbon dioxide from the atmosphere, but at the same time people are cutting down vast areas of these forests. Why is this harmful?

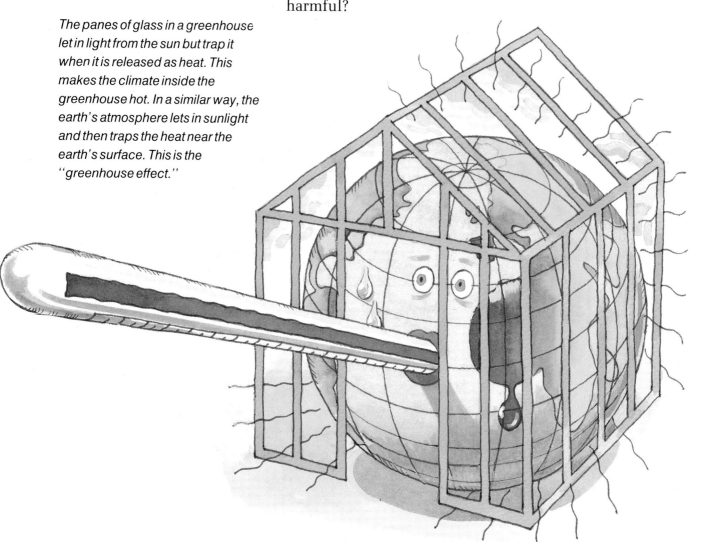

The panes of glass in a greenhouse let in light from the sun but trap it when it is released as heat. This makes the climate inside the greenhouse hot. In a similar way, the earth's atmosphere lets in sunlight and then traps the heat near the earth's surface. This is the "greenhouse effect."

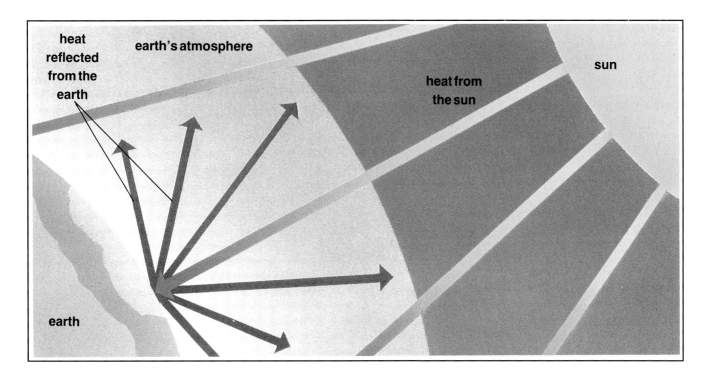

The greenhouse effect

The earth is warmed by the sun. Most of the heat is sent back, or **radiated,** into the atmosphere. Carbon dioxide in the atmosphere traps some of this heat, preventing it from escaping into space. This keeps the earth warm. But if there is too much carbon dioxide in the atmosphere, it will trap too much heat, and the earth's atmosphere will become too hot.

What could happen?

If the earth's atmosphere becomes much warmer, the ice in the Arctic and in Antarctica will begin to melt. This will raise the level of the seas all over the world. A rise of only a few inches could flood many coastlines. Low-lying coastal towns and cities would be endangered by floods, and so would large areas of farmland. If the seas became warmer, the sea animals and plants would be affected. And many might not be able to survive at all. In other parts of the world, a lack of rain may mean that farmland would become too dry and dusty.

Too much carbon dioxide in the atmosphere prevents more heat than usual from escaping into space. But we still need some heat to keep us warm.

Farming the land

Day by day, there are more and more people to be fed. Farming produces most of the food that is needed. In many parts of the world, such as the open grasslands of the United States, Russia, Canada, and Australia, huge areas are plowed and planted with crops, year after year. This kind of farming is called **intensive agriculture.**

Intensive agriculture produces huge harvests for only a few years. Farmers grow the same crop every year. The crops need substances called **nutrients** found in the soil to grow. In time, the growing plants use up the soil's nutrients. Fertilizers are added, but the soil still becomes worn out. Trees and hedgerows that divided the fields thin out and die. The soil is then more easily swept away by strong winds and rain.

Spreading disease

Some pests feed on one particular crop. If the same crop is planted each year, the pests will thrive. They often carry diseases to the new crop. If different crops are planted each year, the pests are not able to feed, and the diseases begin to die out.

Crops, such as corn, can be ruined by disease.

Intensive farming produces huge harvests for a few years. Combine harvesters gather tons of grain from enormous fields.

When too many cattle graze on the land, the grass cannot grow and the soil is easily swept away by the wind and rain.

Damaging the land

Some areas of grassland are not used for growing crops. Farmers often rear sheep or cattle here instead. These animals will provide us with food, but first we must feed them. Some cattle are fed with corn and specially prepared feeds. Some cattle graze the land. Cattle which are kept for beef can eat over 37 pounds (17 kilograms) of feed each day.

There are 1.25 billion cattle in the world. Imagine how much grass they are eating. This can be a problem in the drier areas of Asia and South America where large herds are kept. Here, intensive cattle farming is damaging the land. The grass on which animals graze needs to be left alone for a while so that it can grow again. If the animals are not moved to new pasture, no grass is left to trap moisture and hold the soil together. The land becomes dry and **over-grazed.** Then the soil can be swept away by the wind and the rain.

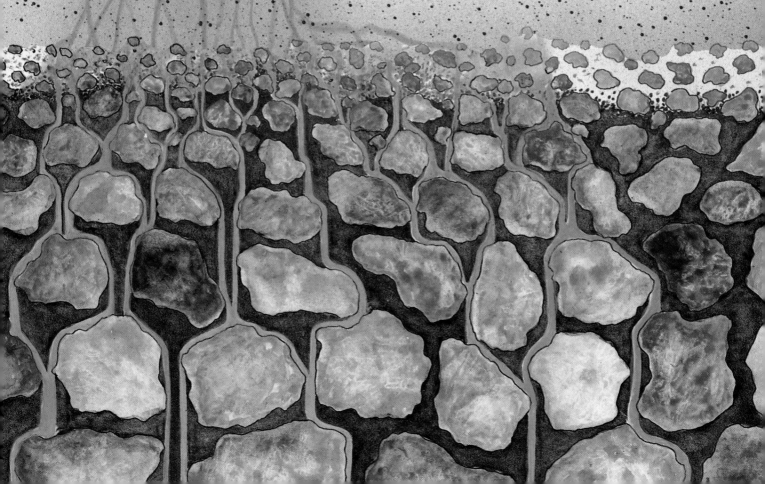

Feeding the land

The farmer has sprayed fertilizer onto his field. Rain falls and washes the fertilizer down into the soil.

After several years, intensive agriculture can leave the soil exhausted. Before the farmer can sow a field with a new crop, the nutrients that have been taken out with the last harvest must be put back. **Chemical fertilizers** may be added to the soil to help the crops grow well.

Weeds and pests

Unwanted weeds growing in the field also take nutrients from the soil. The farmer may use a **chemical weedkiller** on a field to get rid of the weeds. **Chemical pesticides** protect the crops from pests and diseases. However, some pests and diseases learn to resist the chemical sprays. So, in time, the farmer needs to spray the crops with stronger pesticides.

Pesticides can also upset the food chain. For example, ladybugs eat aphids. If a farmer sprays his crops to kill aphids, the ladybugs will not be killed by the pesticide. However, the ladybugs might starve and die because there won't be any aphids to eat.

What happens to the chemicals?

Chemicals are often sprayed on fields from a tractor or an airplane. Some of the chemicals are poisonous to people. If a spray is spread by the wind to nearby houses, it may cause sickness or skin disease.

Chemicals are taken in by plants and so find their way into the food we eat. Some chemicals are washed through the soil into streams and rivers, where they can poison the wildlife. Sometimes, chemicals reach our reservoirs and are pumped to our homes in the water supply.

Careless crop spraying from the air can damage neighboring fields and poison wildlife and people. Crop spraying from the ground is usually safer.

Looking after the land

The land that we need for growing food is very important.
We can't afford to spoil it. There are many ways in which
farmers could make better use of the land and grow good
crops without the help of factory-made chemicals. If it is
farmed with care, the land will go on giving us enough food
to eat for thousands of years to come.

You will need:

three small plant pots

three saucers

some soil

sand

powdered clay

nine beans

three labels

water

notebook and pencil

Testing your soil

Try this experiment to see how well the same kind of plant
grows in different types of soil.

1. Fill the first pot with soil. Fill the
second pot with a mixture of soil and
powdered clay. In the third pot, put a
mixture of soil and sand.

2. Use your pencil to make three
small holes in the soil of each pot.
Drop a bean into each hole and
cover it lightly with soil. Label the
pots and water them every day.

3. When the seedlings begin to
grow, measure their height, count
the number of leaves and look at
their color. Record your
observations in your notebook.

Crop rotation

One method of careful farming is called **crop rotation.**
Different kinds of plants take different nutrients from the soil
and leave others behind. The same crop planted year after
year takes out the same nutrients. But different crops, like
corn and alfalfa, can be planted on the same piece of land. One
year, corn is planted. This will take out certain nutrients from
the soil. The following year, alfalfa will be planted. The alfalfa
will put back the nutrients absorbed by the corn.

Alley cropping

Another farming method is to mix trees and crops on the same
piece of land. In Africa, this is called **alley cropping.** Rows of
quick-growing, deep-rooted trees are planted a few yards
apart, with rows of crops such as sorghum in between. The
trees help to prevent the soil from being blown or washed
away. Their leaves rot and add to the **humus** in the soil.
Humus is made from dead plant matter. Tree shoots provide
animal food and fuel for cooking. The trees and the sorghum
take different nutrients from the soil, so they can grow side by
side.

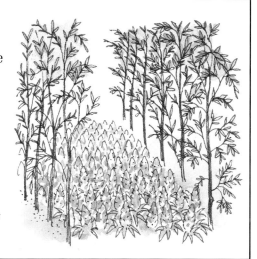

Contour plowing

Sometimes, surface soil, or **topsoil,** is washed away by rain.
This is called **water erosion.** Farmers can help prevent water
erosion by plowing across a slope instead of up and down it.
This is called **contour plowing.** If it rains, water does not run
down the hill, washing away soil as it goes. Instead, it is
caught in the furrows and soaks in, leaving the soil behind.
Contour plowing also prevents streams from getting blocked
by washed-away soil, thus flooding low-lying land.

When land is over-farmed or over-grazed, the topsoil turns to dust, which blows away in the wind. The layer of soil left behind is baked hard by the sun. In time, it cracks. Any rain that falls cannot soak in and flows away.

Spreading deserts

Until about 6,000 years ago, the Sahara in northern Africa was a fertile plain. Many animals roamed across the grassland. There were also many people, herding their animals from pasture to pasture or farming the land. Then the climate began to change. Less rain fell, and the dry land turned to desert.

Today, the Sahara is the earth's largest desert. And it is growing in size every year.

Why does the land turn to desert?

About one-fifth of the earth's land area is desert. Each year, these desert areas of the world are becoming larger. As the soil dries up, the edges of the desert spread and the land can no longer provide food for grazing animals. This is caused partly by changes in the world's climate. But it is made worse by people who have dug up the grassland for farming or allowed too many animals to graze on it.

The moving sands

One of the areas where the desert has spread recently is the Sahel, an area south of the Sahara, in Africa. It is an area of grassland which has often suffered from **drought,** long periods of no rain. Since 1968, the Sahel has suffered from especially bad drought, as well as changes in the climate. The land has dried up and has begun to turn into desert. **Over-grazing** has created more bare soil.

New wells were dug, but the surrounding land was grazed bare as people gathered with their animals. New crops were introduced and fields were no longer left to rest. The few remaining trees were cut down to be used for fuel. Winds from the Sahara blew away the dry topsoil of the Sahel and left barren sand. In the end, there was not enough grassland left to support the people who lived there. Some moved away, but millions of people and animals died in the years after 1968.

How the Sahel became a desert

1. When the Sahel was grassland, it could support a small number of farmers. When the drought became worse, people settled near wells. They cut the trees for fuel. Their animals cleared the grass and trampled the soil.

2. As the population increased, more land was cleared. New crops were grown, which did not allow the soil to rest and regain its nutrients.

3. Winds from the Sahara brought sandstorms, which covered the dry, dusty Sahel soil with sand. People who could not move away with their animals slowly starved.

40

Find out more by looking at pages **42–43**

Fresh air?

How fresh is the air where you live? If you live in the countryside, it might be clean and fresh. All living things must have fresh air to live. Air contains oxygen, which people and animals need, and carbon dioxide, which plants use to make energy from sunlight. There are small amounts of other gases in the air, too, but these are harmless to us.

However, in and near our towns and cities, the air contains many other substances that can harm us. One of these is **sulfur dioxide,** which comes from burning some types of coal and oil. Sulfur dioxide is often an ingredient in another type of air pollution, called **smog.** Smog can build up over an area and cause illness and even death. Small bits of solid or liquid matter that pollute the air are called **particulates.**

What causes most pollution? Although some natural substances, such as dust, pollen, and ash, pollute the air, people create by far most of the harmful pollutants. Power plants that burn coal and oil to produce energy churn out huge amounts of pollution. Factories, the burning of wastes, and the use of chemicals also add to the problem.

Traffic fumes

One of the main causes of air pollution is exhaust fumes from cars and other vehicles that run on gasoline. When gasoline or diesel oil burns, it produces a number of harmful chemicals, such as **nitrogen oxide** and a poisonous gas called **carbon monoxide.** Exhaust fumes also contain a group of chemicals called **hydrocarbons.** Some scientists believe hydrocarbons can cause cancer and other illnesses.

The problems of lead

Until a few years ago, lead was added to most gasolines to make car engines run better. The lead passes through the engine and out of the exhaust system into the air. Lead is poisonous. Breathing in lead-polluted air over a long period of time can cause brain damage.

Reducing air pollution

Though air pollution is still a serious problem, many countries are working to reduce it. Many electric power plants, factories, and facilities that burn wastes are equipped with devices called **scrubbers.** Scrubbers remove sulfur dioxide and other pollutants before the wastes are released into the air.

Governments also have passed regulations to cut down on the pollution from automobiles. For example, the United States has phased out the use of leaded gas, and many countries have banned it altogether. Today's cars are designed to create less pollution. Many are equipped with anti-pollution devices called **catalytic converters,** which reduce the amount of pollution from automobile engines.

Acid rain

Poisonous gases and other chemicals pour into the atmosphere every day. These are the waste products from our power stations, factories, and cars. Two of these waste gases, sulfur dioxide and nitrogen oxide, collect in the atmosphere. They then mix with the moisture in the air to become **sulfuric acid** and **nitric acid.** These acids are absorbed by rain clouds and fall to the ground again as **acid rain.** The acid rain clouds can drift hundreds of miles before falling as rain. Acid rain can fall a long way from the place where the gases first entered the atmosphere.

Where does acid rain fall?

The areas where most acid rain falls are the eastern part of North America, central and northwestern Europe, and parts of Asia. Acid rain falling on North America comes from the industrial cities of the United States. Much of the acid rain in northwestern Europe has drifted from Germany.

Sulfur dioxide and nitrogen oxide from coal-fired power stations and factory chimneys are causes of acid rain.

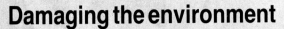

Damaging the environment

Acid rain can cause serious damage. It kills trees and destroys many wildlife habitats. Areas of forest in eastern North America, central Europe, and parts of Asia have been damaged by acid rain.

When acid rain falls into lakes and rivers, it harms the fish, plants, and other freshwater life. In cities, acid rain can even eat away at the stonework of buildings.

How can we prevent acid rain?

Acid rain passes from one country to another. The problem of acid rain can only be solved by agreements between countries. About 20 countries have already agreed to cut down the pollution that causes acid rain. They have agreed to control fumes from power stations and factories.

Waste gases from power stations and factory chimneys rise into the air. The gases mix with water vapor in the clouds.

These clouds are carried great distances by the wind. The rain which falls from them is a weak acid. This acid rain damages the countryside.

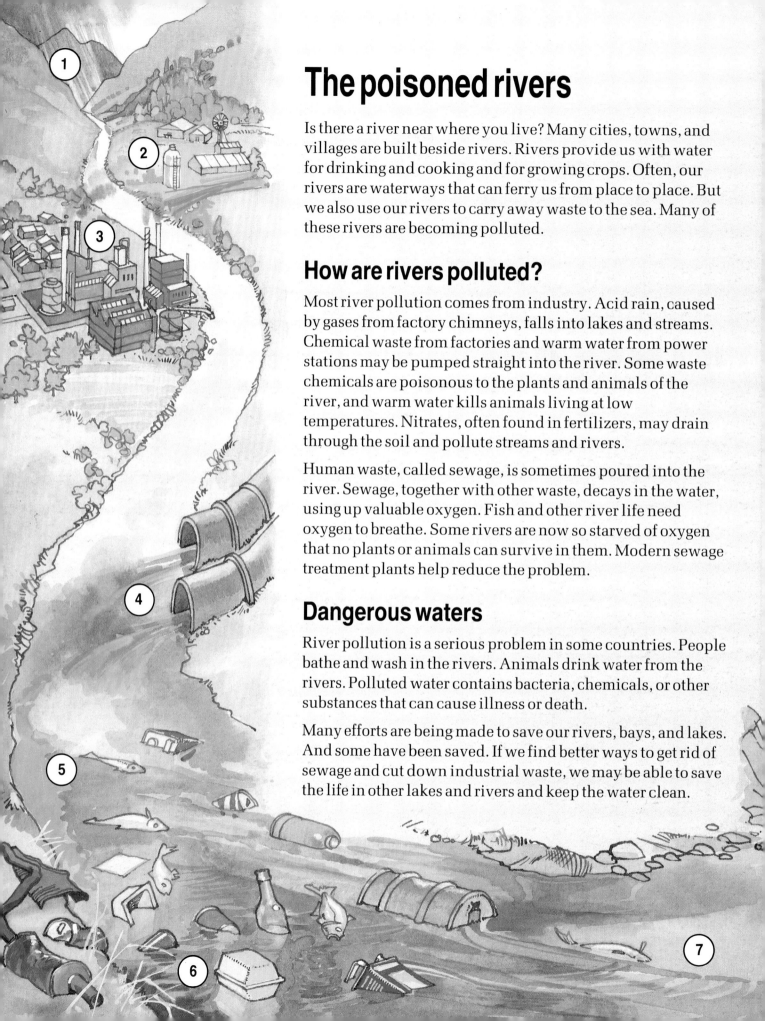

The poisoned rivers

Is there a river near where you live? Many cities, towns, and villages are built beside rivers. Rivers provide us with water for drinking and cooking and for growing crops. Often, our rivers are waterways that can ferry us from place to place. But we also use our rivers to carry away waste to the sea. Many of these rivers are becoming polluted.

How are rivers polluted?

Most river pollution comes from industry. Acid rain, caused by gases from factory chimneys, falls into lakes and streams. Chemical waste from factories and warm water from power stations may be pumped straight into the river. Some waste chemicals are poisonous to the plants and animals of the river, and warm water kills animals living at low temperatures. Nitrates, often found in fertilizers, may drain through the soil and pollute streams and rivers.

Human waste, called sewage, is sometimes poured into the river. Sewage, together with other waste, decays in the water, using up valuable oxygen. Fish and other river life need oxygen to breathe. Some rivers are now so starved of oxygen that no plants or animals can survive in them. Modern sewage treatment plants help reduce the problem.

Dangerous waters

River pollution is a serious problem in some countries. People bathe and wash in the rivers. Animals drink water from the rivers. Polluted water contains bacteria, chemicals, or other substances that can cause illness or death.

Many efforts are being made to save our rivers, bays, and lakes. And some have been saved. If we find better ways to get rid of sewage and cut down industrial waste, we may be able to save the life in other lakes and rivers and keep the water clean.

The river's journey

This river is clean when it starts its journey to the sea. Many plants and fish live in the water.

1. Rain clouds carry acid rain from the towns on the other side of the mountains. The acid rain falls in the streams that feed the river.

2. The river passes a farm where chemicals are washed into it by the rain.

3. Farther on, the river passes a town where it is polluted with chemicals from factories.

4. Then sewage enters the river and decays. Foam comes from detergents which the sewage system has been unable to break down.

5. By this time, all the fish have been poisoned. There are no plants on the river bank either.

6. People see that the river is a dump and throw even more garbage into it.

7. By the time the water reaches the sea, it's in a terrible mess!

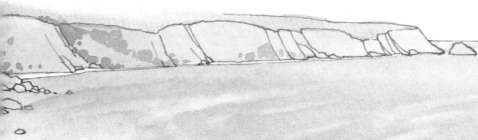

Waste from copper mines has turned the water of the Rio Tinto in Spain deep red. People have mined near this river for thousands of years. Its name means "colored river."

Find out more by looking at pages **44 – 45**

The dirty oceans

You probably think our oceans are so huge that they could never become badly polluted. Unfortunately, this is not the case. At the end of a river's journey, it will dump all its pollution into the sea. This pollution can kill or drive away sea creatures that live near river mouths and coasts. The sea can also be polluted by container ships that carry garbage and waste materials from factories. The ships dump their poisonous cargo into the ocean.

Oil spillage

Some of the worst sea pollution comes from modern supertankers, which are over 1,500 feet (457 meters) long. They carry more than 500,000 short tons (450,000 metric tons) of oil. If a supertanker runs aground or breaks up in rough seas, it quickly creates a major disaster as the oil spills over the surface of the sea.

Coastal oil spills are especially harmful, killing fish, sea birds, and other sea animals. Oil clogs their scales and feathers so that they cannot move. Birds often swallow the poisonous oil when they try to clean it from their feathers.

This bird can't fly because its feathers are covered in oil. Although rescuers try to clean off the oil, many birds die in oil spills.

Garbage thrown overboard from ships litters the shoreline.

Household waste, called sewage, drains into the ocean.

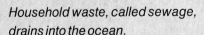

Poisoning the food chain

Fish that live in the sea take in chemicals from polluted sea water and poisoned plants. If the fish survive, they may be eaten by other animals. In turn, these animals will be poisoned. The poison is carried through the food chain.

Tiny living creatures called bacteria in sewage and other waste products quickly multiply in the sea. The bacteria use up valuable oxygen in the water. Fish and other sea animals need oxygen to breathe. They will soon die from lack of oxygen if the sea water becomes too polluted.

Dangerous wastes from industry are dumped at sea in containers. The containers may decay one day and release their poisons into the water.

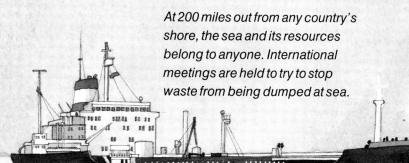

At 200 miles out from any country's shore, the sea and its resources belong to anyone. International meetings are held to try to stop waste from being dumped at sea.

Cleaning up the water

Oil spills are often broken up using detergents. Try this for yourself.

You will need:

some oil

household detergent

a screw-top jar filled with water

1. Add a few drops of oil to the jar of water. Screw on the lid and give the jar a shake. Has the oil mixed with the water?

2. Now add a few drops of detergent to the jar. Screw the lid back on and shake the jar well. What has happened to the oil?

Find out more by looking at pages **50–51**

Explosion at Chernobyl

Nuclear power stations use a radioactive material called uranium as an energy source to make electricity. Radioactive materials give out energy called **radiation.** It is a very powerful form of energy that is absorbed by everything around it. Plants, animals, and people are affected by radiation. It attacks the cells which make up our bodies. Radiation energy remains active for a long time.

Early in the morning of April 26, 1986, alarm bells began to ring at a poorly constructed power station at Chernobyl in what is now Ukraine. Soon after, there was an explosion and fire at the power station, which sent a dangerous cloud of radioactive material into the air. As a result, many living things were exposed to dangerous levels of radiation.

Radioactive clouds swept across many parts of Europe during the days following the explosion at Chernobyl.

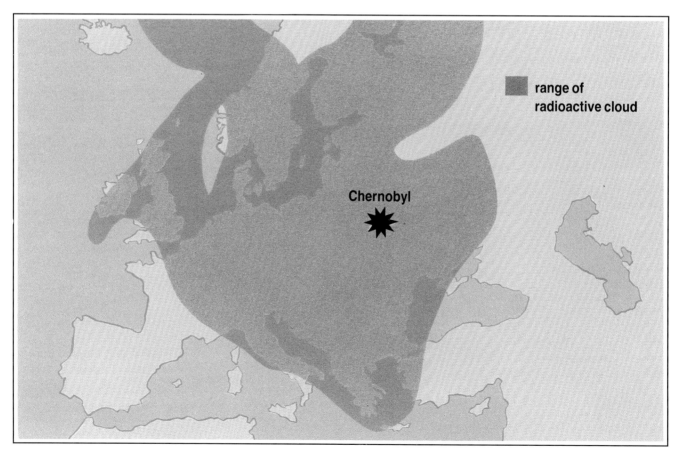

range of radioactive cloud

Chernobyl

The power station at Chernobyl was destroyed by the accident.

Scientists wearing safety clothing used Geiger counters to measure levels of radioactivity in the countryside surrounding Chernobyl.

Widespread and long-lasting damage

For a few days after the explosion, wind spread the radioactive cloud over central and northwestern Europe. Some people died as a result of the accident, and many people were seriously injured. Others are still suffering from the effects of radiation sickness. Radioactive rain fell on land on which animals were grazing. After the accident, animals that had eaten radioactive grass could not be used for milk or meat. Many more people will probably die or become ill from the radioactivity, which will remain active for many years.

The world needs electricity. Nuclear power is one way of producing it. But what if there is another, even more serious accident? Such accidents are possible, even at power plants better constructed than the one at Chernobyl.

Nuclear dump

Nuclear energy is useful. We can make electricity from radioactive material in nuclear power stations. In hospitals, radioactivity can help to cure some diseases. In some industries, people use radioactive processes to measure and test materials.

Radioactive material produces waste, which may be in the form of a gas, a liquid, or a solid. This waste can't simply be thrown away like other waste. It is dangerous because it continues to emit radiation. Some of it, called **high-level waste,** will be radioactive for thousands of years. **Low-level waste** is less radioactive, but scientists do not agree on how dangerous it is.

Closing power stations

Nuclear power stations don't last forever. They become old and worn out. When this happens, a huge amount of nuclear waste created in the station is left behind. It will still be dangerous for many, many years. What can we do with this radioactive waste? One answer seems to be to put a thick case of concrete around it.

This is the international symbol showing that a container has radioactive material in it. If you ever see anything with this mark on it lying around, keep away from it and report it to the police.

This reprocessing plant at Sellafield in England recovers radioactive material from nuclear waste. Some low-level waste is pumped into the Irish Sea.

What happens to nuclear waste?

The waste from nuclear power stations in the United Kingdom and France is sent to a nuclear reprocessing plant. The waste is then separated into different radioactive parts. Valuable fuel and other materials are recovered. Some low-level waste is pumped straight into the sea. Other low-level waste is buried. High-level waste is sealed in concrete and steel tanks and stored deep underground or underwater.

Living with nuclear waste

It is difficult to find sites where large amounts of nuclear waste can be dumped safely. Few people want to live near a **nuclear dump.** We cannot be sure that the waste containers will not break up and leak. What would happen to them if there was an earthquake? And what if an underwater container leaked and let large amounts of radioactivity pass into the sea?

Sometimes, nuclear waste is carried from a power station by rail.

The waste-makers

Who are the champion waste-makers of the world? This garbage pile shows the relative amount of household waste each of these countries throws away in a year. The USA is top of the heap — it produces more garbage than any other country in the world.

Can you imagine how much garbage we create all over the world each day? In factories, offices, hotels, and restaurants, as well as in our homes, we produce tons of garbage. Over a year, this builds up into a huge problem. Many poorer countries of the world produce the smallest amounts of garbage. In countries where there are many industries, more land is needed for garbage sites. Some of our garbage can be used again. But where can we put the rest? No one wants a garbage dump next door!

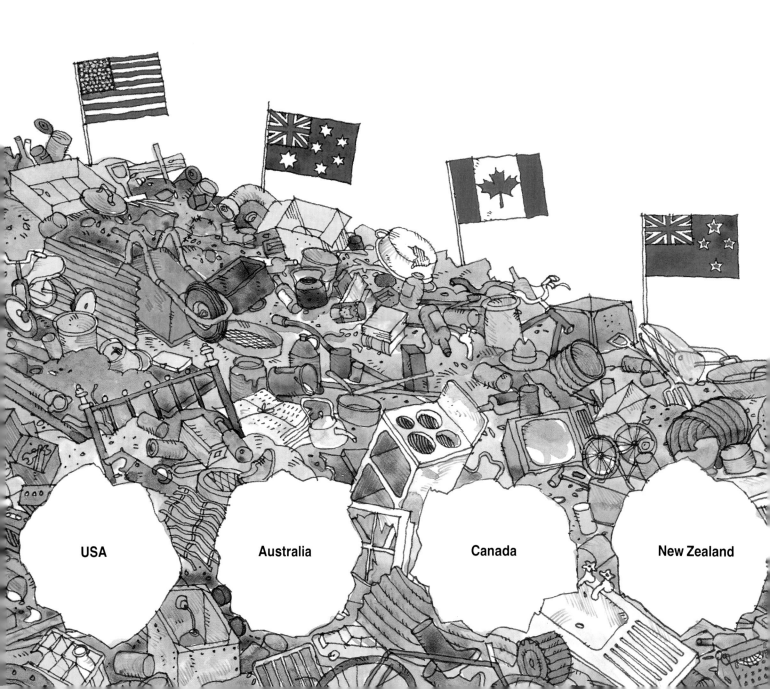

USA

Australia

Canada

New Zealand

Industrial waste

Waste can be burnt, but this can pollute the atmosphere. It can be dumped at sea, but this pollutes the sea. There is no way of getting rid of waste that does not harm the environment in some way. Much of the waste is made in factories. When coal or other minerals are mined, waste in the form of stone and dust is brought to the surface. This is usually dumped on land in mountainous heaps, which look ugly. The heaps can sometimes cause dangerous landslides. Other waste, produced by factories making chemicals and plastics, is poisonous. Liquid waste from factories is one of the main causes of river and lake pollution.

Waste space

Garbage must be put somewhere. Most of it is buried in old quarries or sites, and this levels out the land. When the site is full, it is covered over and often used as a building site. But that is not the end of the story. Underground, the rubbish breaks down and decays. It produces an explosive, poisonous gas called **methane.** This may escape to the surface. Rotting garbage can seep into the ground and pollute water supplies.

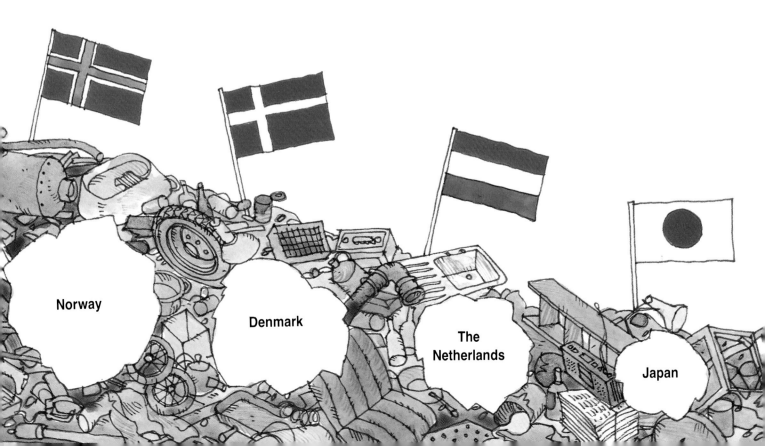

Norway

Denmark

The Netherlands

Japan

54

Find out more by looking at
pages **52–53**
56–57

Useful garbage

We make objects like paper, bottles, and cans, and then we throw them away! As time goes on, we are building up more and more garbage, which is hard to get rid of. There would be much less garbage if we saved some of the waste materials and used them again. This would also save energy because large amounts of energy are used in making new products.

New products from old

Have you ever wondered what happens to all the things we put in the garbage can? Cans, bottles, jars, cartons, newspapers, magazines, plastics, old clothes, old toys, old furniture—we throw away loads of them each year. Most of our household garbage could be used again. This is called **recycling.** Waste such as coffee grounds, potato peels and other vegetable scraps will decay in time and can be turned into **compost.** This is a natural fertilizer for garden plants. Old paper, metal, and glass can also be broken up and remade.

Here are the contents of a typical family garbage can.

The newspapers can be put to one side for recycling. The jars and bottles can be taken to the recycling bin. The cans may be melted down and the metal used again.

The kitchen scraps can be put on the compost heap. That will leave only about one-fifth of the waste in the garbage can.

When you use a recycling bin, put the glass in the correct containers for the different colors. Take caps and lids off.

What about plastics?

Plastics create one of our worst waste problems. They are more difficult to recycle, because there are so many different types of plastic. Most plastics are **nonbiodegradable,** which means that they take a very long time before they begin to decay. Often, we use plastics when we don't need to. We buy food in a plastic container and then throw the container away as soon as we are home. Now scientists are trying to make machines that will sort out the different plastics and melt them down for reuse.

Some new types of plastic are **biodegradable.** Once they have been thrown away, they eventually decay. They can even be used for compost. If we changed over to this kind of plastic packaging, there would be less litter in the streets. And we wouldn't have to dispose of so many unwanted plastics.

How is waste recycled?

When you recycle materials, you are helping conservation in three ways. You are helping to keep down damage caused to the environment by cutting down trees or by mining for raw materials. You are helping to save energy. You are also helping to cut down the problems of waste disposal.

Paper

Most paper is made from wood pulp, which comes from trees. Whole forests have to be cut down to provide us with newspapers. That is bad enough, but large amounts of energy are used to turn the wood pulp into paper and to bleach it to make the paper white. This process releases chemicals into our rivers and so causes water pollution.

Recycled paper must first have the ink taken out. It is then turned into pulp and pressed back into sheets of paper. Recycled paper is as good as new paper, although it is a little rougher and not as white. Only about one-quarter of the world's paper is recycled. At least another quarter could be saved. Paper can also be recycled and used to make papier mâché.

Glass

Huge amounts of energy are used in making glass, because very high temperatures are needed to melt down all the ingredients. If bottles and jars are thrown away when they are empty, all that energy is lost. But new bottles and jars can be made out of a mixture of new glass and old, broken glass, which is called cullet. This saves up to one-quarter of the energy needed to make new glass.

Metals

Metal cans are made of aluminum, or steel coated with tin, or a mixture of these metals. Aluminum cans are the most valuable to recycle. In the United States, over half of all aluminum cans are recycled. Aluminum is made from an ore called **bauxite,** which has to be electrically heated to a high temperature. Recycling saves 95 per cent of the energy needed to make new aluminum cans.

Recycling paper

Paper is quite easy to recycle. Try to do it for yourself.

You will need:

some used construction paper or newspaper

a cloth

a fork

some water

a saucepan

a large bowl

a flat-bottomed sieve

1. Tear the paper into small pieces and put them into a saucepan. Fill the saucepan halfway with water. Leave the paper to soak overnight.

2. If the paper has soaked up all the water, add some more. Mash the soggy paper with a fork until it has broken up into a mushy pulp.

3. Fill the bowl halfway with water and add two handfuls of paper pulp. Stir the mixture well. Put a damp cloth beside the bowl.

4. Dip your sieve upside down under the water and bring it up. Hold it above the bowl until most of the water has drained away.

5. Turn the sieve right side up on the damp cloth and rock the sieve gently back and forth until the paper pulp peels away.

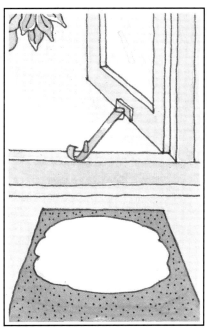

6. Spread the pulp as thinly and as evenly as possible over the cloth. Leave the pulp in an airy place to dry.

The Green family

Everyone can help with conservation. The Green family, who live in this house, have thought carefully about saving energy. This means that they also save money — and eat healthier food, too. Not many families can take all these steps, but all of us can do something to help.

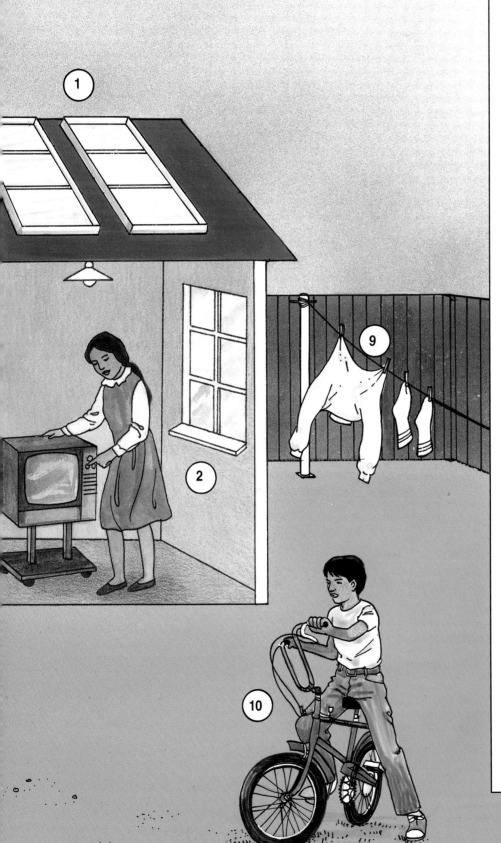

1. Solar panels on the roof collect heat from the sun. These provide the house with hot water.

2. Windows are double-glazed to keep the heat in when it is cold, and to keep the house cool in hot weather.

3. Insulation around the hot water tank prevents heat from escaping.

4. Lights are switched off in rooms not being used.

5. Dripping faucets waste water. All the faucets turn off properly.

6. Homemade jams and pickles are cheaper and healthier than store-bought ones. The jars can be used again and again.

7. Separate cans are used for organic waste, paper, glass, aluminum, and other garbage.

8. Organic waste is used for compost.

9. Laundry is dried in the open air instead of in an electric drier. This saves energy.

10. Bicycles are used instead of the car for short journeys, to save gasoline.

11. This car runs on unleaded gasoline to help keep the air clean.

The green land

In this green land, the people are doing all they can to conserve the earth's resources.

Used glass, metals, and paper are collected so that they can be recycled.

River and sea water are not polluted and are safe for swimming and other water sports.

Farm animals are kept outside instead of in factory farms. They are fed partly on feed made from organic waste.

Farmers rotate their crops. This helps to keep the soil fertile, and fewer chemical fertilizers are needed.

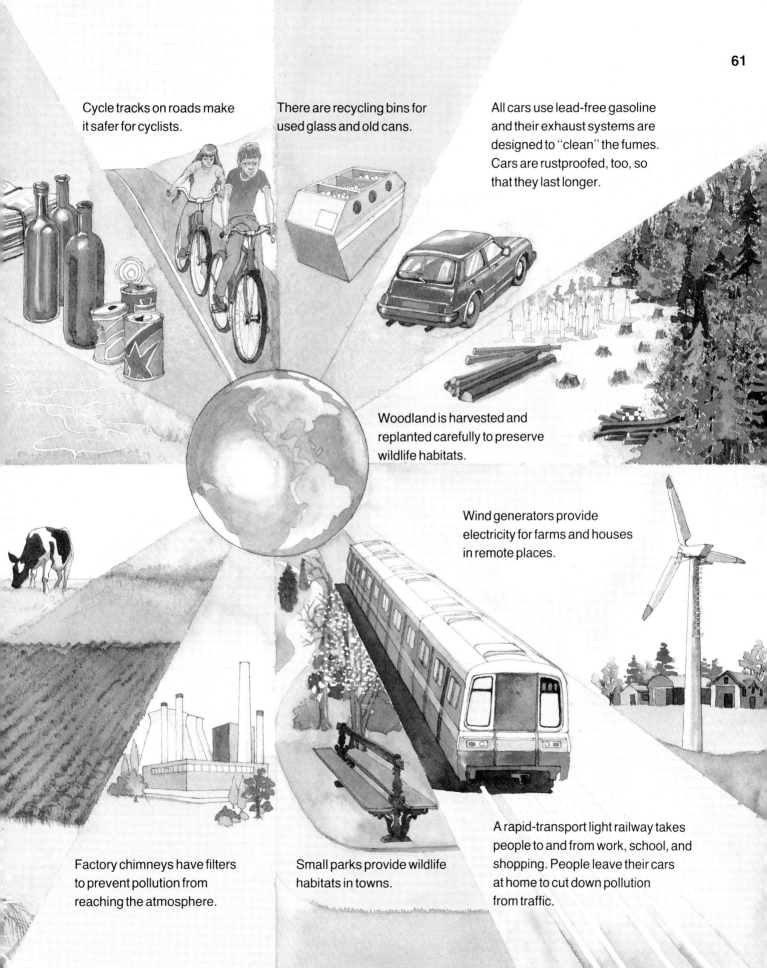

Cycle tracks on roads make it safer for cyclists.

There are recycling bins for used glass and old cans.

All cars use lead-free gasoline and their exhaust systems are designed to "clean" the fumes. Cars are rustproofed, too, so that they last longer.

Woodland is harvested and replanted carefully to preserve wildlife habitats.

Wind generators provide electricity for farms and houses in remote places.

Factory chimneys have filters to prevent pollution from reaching the atmosphere.

Small parks provide wildlife habitats in towns.

A rapid-transport light railway takes people to and from work, school, and shopping. People leave their cars at home to cut down pollution from traffic.

Glossary

Acid rain:
Substance that forms when moisture in the air combines with certain chemicals released by automobiles, factories, and power plants that burn coal or oil. This substance falls to the earth with rain or snow.

Alley cropping:
Farming method by which trees and crops are mixed on the same piece of land.

Biodegradable:
Able to decay.

Chlorofluorocarbon:
Harmful chemical used in aerosol cans that causes substances, such as polish or deodorant, to shoot out of the can.

Coal:
Black substance that forms in the earth from matter that has decayed.

Compost:
Natural fertilizer made from waste. It is used to help garden plants grow.

Conservation:
Careful use of something, especially a natural resource, to help save the earth and its resources.

Contour plowing:
Farming method by which crops are plowed across a slope instead of up and down it. This helps prevent the wearing away of the soil by water.

Crop rotation:
Farming method by which different crops are planted on the same piece of land at different times.

Drought:
Long period of no rain.

Endangered species:
Animal group in danger of dying out.

Fertilizer:
Substance added to soil to help crops grow well.

Greenhouse effect:
Behavior of the earth's atmosphere that causes heat from the sun to be trapped near the earth's surface.

Habitat:
Home to many living things, both plants and animals.

Humus:
Substance made from dead plant matter.

Intensive agriculture:
Farming method by which huge areas of land are plowed and planted with crops year after year.

Natural resource:
Something that the earth provides.

Nutrient:
Substance that living things need to grow and survive.

Ozone layer:
Layer of gas that surrounds the earth. Ozone shields the earth from some of the dangerous rays of the sun.

Pesticide:
Special liquid used to protect farm crops from pests and diseases.

Poacher:
Illegal hunter of endangered animals.

Radiation:
Energy given out by *radioactive* materials. It is a very powerful form of energy that is absorbed by everything around it.

Radioactive:
Having energy that is created by atoms breaking up.

Recycling:
Process by which waste is used again.

Solar panel:
Glass-topped box fixed to the roof of a building, facing the sun. The inside of the box is painted black. Black is best at taking in, or absorbing, heat. Water flows through pipes inside the box. During daylight, this water is heated by the sun's energy.

Tropical rain forest:
Huge, dense forest where it is hot and wet. Trees and plants grow very quickly in a tropical rain forest.

Ultraviolet ray:
Invisible form of light. The sun is the major source of ultraviolet rays.

Index